T0194945

Through Sunlight and Showers

Kathy Austin

authorHOUSE®

AuthorHouse™
1663 Liberty Drive
Bloomington, IN 47403
www.authorhouse.com
Phone: 1 (800) 839-8640

Published by AuthorHouse 06/13/2019

ISBN: 978-1-7283-1577-5 (sc)
ISBN: 978-1-7283-1576-8 (e)

Contents

Poetry of Prayer

About The Author...

I was born in upstate New York, on July 6th, 1955. My parents were everyday working people, and weren't what you would call overly spiritual. I am the youngest of two girls. My childhood was rather uneventful, although I always had a fascination about God, and often found myself "playing church" with my dolls. My father and I were baptized together, when I was nine years old, in a private ceremony of a local church sanctuary. I have always remembered that night, and know deep in my heart, that God made me His own at that time.

When I was a teen, in the sixties, my time was spent caught up in the hippie movement. I honestly felt that I was born exactly when I should have been, as I had to change nothing about myself to fit in. My involvement in civil rights activities, and concern for getting our troops out of Viet Nam was very strong, and the "Jesus Movement" came along at just the right time for me. Although I strayed from time to time away from my walk with the Lord, He has never allowed me to wander too far off of His path for my life. Whenever I was finished dabbling in the worldly aspects of life, He always welcomed me home as He would any prodigal son.

Through good times and bad, triumphs and tragedies, Jesus has been by my side, and has blessed me with a loving, supportive family, to see me through some very dark hours. Everything that I am, everything that I have, belongs to Him, and I give Him all of the praise and honor and glory. In Christian Love, Kathy.

Foreword

Why is it so terribly easy to praise God in the good times, and yet, so difficult to do so in the bad?

After all, when we need Him the most, (although I find my need of Him to be constant), He is right there, waiting for us to call upon Him. How many people in your life, are on-call for you 24/7? How many people do you know, who would be willing to listen to your constant cries and complaints? I can't think of too many. But Jesus is always willing. And, He has never yet said to me: "I told you so," or "quit your whining, you have life so easy compared to what I endured for you!"

This book is about those times. Good times, and bad ones. When I rejoice in His goodness, I sing praises to Him for His unfailing love for me. When I am suffering, (as I see suffering), I cry out to Him in my pain, but thank Him and praise Him for His tender mercies toward me. He is my life, my master, my savior, and my very best friend. I heard it once said that, a friend is someone who knows all about you, but loves you anyway. Jesus is just that kind of friend.

If you do not have a personal relationship with Him now, I invited you and encourage you to invite Him into your heart, now today. Simply tell Him that you have wandered away and that you cannot run your life by yourself anymore. Ask Him to forgive you, to accept you, to love you. You will be welcomed into His fold with open arms, and your life will never be the same! If you have made this decision for Christ, I would love to hear from you. I would love to pray 'with you, and for you. Please send me an E-mail letting me know that you belong to the Lord now, and I will gladly welcome you as my new brother or sister in the Lord. I truly hope that you will find comfort, hope, and renewed strength in my writings.

While the majority of the poetry upon these pages is about praising and praying to our wonderful Father and redeemer, I have included a few that are just about life in general. When I get sentimental, or romantic, or silly, I just call it, "me being me." I have often been misunderstood by those around me, walking to the "beat of a different drummer" has been my way for a life time, and I would not change a thing that I have ever seen, felt or experienced. May the Lord richly bless you, in all that you do. Just stay focused on Him, giving Him the "first fruits" of all that you do, and His love will shine upon you, and all whom you come into contact with.

Love and Prayers,
Kathy

Poetry of Praise

And He said to me:" My grace is sufficient for thee,
for My strength is made perfect in weakness."
Most gladly then, will I rather glory in my
infirmities, that the power of Christ may
rest upon me. Therefore I take pleasure
in infirmities, in reproaches, in
necessities, in persecutions,
in distresses for His sake.
For when I am weak,
then am I strong.
2 Cor. 12:9-10

Through Sunlight And Showers

When I am my weakest,
I feel my greatest strength.
The Lord flexes. His muscles,
to give my faith more length.

Though my heart fills with sorrow,
and I can't see through the tears,
I have witnessed so much growth,
in me, through out the years.

Often persecuted,
for speaking the Lords' truth,
I have been kepi protected,
from the trials of my youth.

The road is long and rocky,
and I've had many falls,
but one thing I am certain of,
He hears my heartfelt calls.

And so we walk together,
through sunlight and the showers,
I will never cease to praise
the Lords' gracious, loving powers.

10/01/02

He Is The Only One

He said I shouldn't worry,
I shouldn't be afraid,
but when I look upon my life,
What a mess I've made.

He gave to me such riches,
wealth beyond compare.
But I feel so empty,
like there is nothing there.

Jesus is the only one,
the only one I need,
He is the one who comforts me,
The one from whom I feed.

Those nail scarred hands reach out to me,
and beckon me come in.
They cleanse and bathe me to my soul,
and take away my Sin.

He said I shouldn't worry,
though sometimes I still do,
and if you go to Him in prayer,
He will comfort you too.

Jesus, Jesus, Jesus,
my faithful and true friend,
I will stay within Your power,
from now until the end.

01/24/04

"My soul glorifies the Lord and my spirit rejoices in God my Savior." Luke 1: 46-4 7

Happy Birthday Jesus!

My soul doth glorify the Lord,
who was born this day for me.
My spirit rejoices in my God,
My Savior has set me free.

Oh lowly one born in the hay,
what gift to us is given!
The one true Lord, of purest love,
brings us the life worth living,

Beneath the stars,
one cold, dark night,
a baby's cry was heard.
It was the God of Heaven,
fulfilling His faithful word.

Angels rejoiced,
the animals bowed,
for they knew from the start,
this miracle of miracles,
straight from the Father's heart.

Happy birthday Jesus!
My soul cries out with glee,
I sing my humble praises,
and offer myself to Thee.

Take from me all sinful things,
and replace them with desire,
to fulfill Your mighty will,
set my heart on fire.

My soul doth glorify the Lord,
draw me near, I pray,
and bring to me, Your blessed peace,
on this fine Christmas Day.

December 17th, 2003

Gods' Light

Matthew 2:10

"When they saw the star, they were filled with joy!"

We see His star,
most any night,
and to me,
'tis a beautiful sight.

This little babe
became our Lord,
and-through the ages,
kept His word.

From earthly strife,
we have no fear,
if to our savior,
we draw near.

Think of it!
Born and died for you!
Fulfilling all of
God's promises true.

When you go out,
on this cold, crisp night,
raise your eyes,
look for that light.

Take a minute
to thank the Lord,
you can take Him,
at His word.

December 16th, 2003

May He grant you your hearts' desire,
and fulfill all your plans.
Psalm 20:4

My Hearts' Desire

He is my hearts' desire
His work my perfect plan.
He cleanses me in fire,
and leads me with His hand.

Though I lived in darkness,
and wandered in despair,
He was ever with me,
and kept me in His care.

Compassionate, He rescued me,
and held me to Hip breast,
He took away my sorrow,
and gave me perfect rest.

I will praise Him all day long
this perfect God and man,
He is my hearts' desire,
His work, my perfect plan.

July 26, 2003

Praises For Promises

Oh, God,
I love this promise
that you have made to me!
Great has your faithfulness been
to me over the years!

Not once,
in all of my hours of darkness,
have you ever
left my side!

Through lost jobs,
lost friendships,
lost babies,
you have held my hand.

Through shaking,
trembling,
and. despair,
you have been with me!

Whether lying down,
or rising up,
whether walking through
darkest night,
or brightest day,
you have walked
shoulder to shoulder,
on life's paths beside me.

I thank you daily, my Father,
that you will
never leave me,
or forsake me.

In Jesus name,
I praise you!
Amen!

07/18/03

Imagine When You Take Me!

What is the way to the place
where the lightening is dispersed,
or the place where the east winds
are scattered over the earth?
Job 38:24

Imagine if You could take me
on a tour of Your vast universe!
I could peek in through the windows
of the house of lightening!

You could show to me
the storehouse of the mighty wind!
And the place where all is made.
Imagine what my heart would feel!

Imagine if You could take me
to visit every star!
Together we would walk the planets
and see beyond what man can see!

One day, this all will happen!
A proud father,
showing his handywork
to all of his children!

"This is now all yours!" You will say.
"I created this for you!" You will boast.
And rightly so!
From Your endless love, this all came to be!

My heart bursts,
to think of that glorious day,
when You take me on that tour,
of Your vast universe.

06/28/03

"What is the way to the abode of light?
And where does the darkness reside?
Can you take them to their places?
Do you know the paths to their dwellings?
Job: 19-20

Only You Know

Only You know, O Father of light,
from whence has come our day.
Only You give rest to Your children,
when the darkness comes forth to play.

You keep these things,
in a secret place,
where none of us may go.

All creation,
has it's space,
That only You God, shall know.

It's not our job,
to wonder where
all of life comes from.

Our job is only
with grateful praise,
to thank you for all You've done.

06/26/03

"Have you ever given orders to the morning,
or shown the dawn it's place,
that it might take the earth by the edges
and shake the wicked ou1 of it?
Job 38:12-13

Praise Be To You!

How powerful You are, O Lord!
That even the morning obeys!
that the sun in evening,
humbly bows in Your presence!

Oh, to be the one
to shake the very earth
into reverent obedience!
Into humble adoration of you.

Even the clouds
part at Your command,
and the birds scatter,
at Your mighty thunderous voice!

Of what shall I be afraid?
For You are my God
and my protector.
Praise be to You, O Lord!

06/26/03

"Who endowed the heart with wisdom,
or gave understanding to the mind?"
Job: 38:36

It Is You!

It is You, almighty God,
who gave us ears to hear,
and mouths to proclaim
Your greatness!

From the sands of the earth
You formed us,
and breathed into us
the breath of life!

It is You, almighty God,
who filled our hearts
with Your magnificent wisdom!

It is You, almighty God,
who gave us a mind
to absorb understanding!

All the days of my life,
will I proclaim Your greatness!
Your love for me
is beyond measure!

06/26/03

A Simple Talk With God

There's so much that I want to do
and always so little time,
many valleys to visit
numerous mountains to climb.

When sailing on life's ocean,
I find myself longing for land.
When we are far apart my Lord,
I constantly seek your hand.

I've crossed many a desert,
wandered the lush greenery,
everywhere I. look, I see,
such beautiful scenery.

Yet when I look on my own life,
so many things I lack.
So I make my way, home to You,
and You always take me back.

Humbly I bow before You,
in thanks for all You have done,
I eagerly wait, my brand new home,
Lord, let Your kingdom come.

11/22/02

*"Oh, the depth of the riches of the wisdom
and knowledge of God!"*
Romans 11:33

The Wisdom and Knowledge of God

God knows all things,
God sees all things,
He watches over me.

He gave His son,
Spared not his life,
to set this captive free.

He is so wise, so wonderful
God knows my every need,
The knowledge of my Lord and God,
Surpasses us indeed!

I feel His hand upon me,
As I travel on,
He lifts my cares; lightens my load,
All of my troubles are gone.

I will praise Him endlessly,
For all that He has done,
I will sing of His graciousness,
from sun to setting sun.

09/13/02 KA

My Hope Is In The Lord, My God

My hope is in the Lord, my God,
creator of the earth.
His hand has been upon my life,
from the moment of my birth.

As a child He spoke to me,
and told me of His plans,
I've not always followed faithfully,
heeding His commands.

Still my. Father waited,
until I returned,
and I am so grateful
for the many lessons learned.

My hope is in the Lord, my God,
forever I shall stay,
following Him faithfully,
until my dying day

09/11/02

In The Still Small Voice

In the still small voice, He beckons me
"Be still, and know I'm God."
He will light my every step,
As I walk upon the sod.

Though my burden sometimes,
Feels too great to bear,
If I sit and listen,
I can hear Him there.

My God, the ruler of my life,
My care taker indeed,
Shall never leave or forsake me,
If the still small voice I heed.

09/11/02

"And they shall mount up on wings as eagles……….."
Isaiah 30:41

Teach Me To Fly!

Oh that you would give me wings,
And teach me how to fly!
Oh that you would give to me,
only happy tears to cry.

I would soar to mountain tops
how happy I would be!
To spend my life in faithfulness,
serving only Thee.

Alas I know, that I must walk;
through valleys dark find cold.
But when you come and rescue me,
I'm showered with riches untold.

And so my Lord, I follow,
and place my trust in Thee,
for I know, that it's your love,
that sets me completely free.

10/01/02

"For I know the plans I have for you,"
declares the Lord, "plans to prosper
you and not to harm you, plans to
give you hope and a future.
Then you will call upon Me
and come and pray and I will listen to you."
Jeremiah 29: 11-12

He Hears My Every Whisper

He hears my every whisper,
He sees my every tear.
He takes away my sorrow,
He calms my every fear.

The Lord gives me great riches,
He heals my broken heart,
The Lord provides my every need,
never shall we part.

We only need to trust Him,
to lead us on the way.
We only need to follow Him,
walking day by day.

And when our journey's over,
how happy we will be,
to live with God in heaven,
we will be truly free.

10/01/02

The Promise

He never promised laughter,
without a little pain,
He never promised sunshine,
without a little rain.

He did promise a rainbow,
after every storm.
And His everlasting love,
to keep me safe and warm.

He never promised riches,
as defined down here on earth,
but He did give me forever,
through His death and my rebirth.

The promises He gave me,
are always coming true,
and if you'll only ask Him,
He'll give them all to you.

07/06/02

"For He satisfies the thirsty, and feeds the hungry good things ..."
Psalm 107:9

He Satisfies me

I came to you in brokenness,
And you made me whole.
I came to you a starving child,
And you filled my empty bowl.

You satisfied my desperate thirst,
And bathed me tenderly,
Now clothed in your forgiveness,
You set me completely free,

Now I choose to follow you,
I praise your mighty name,
For you have satisfied me,
When into my life you came.

10/01/02

When the cares of my heart are many,
Your consolations cheer my soul! Psalm 94:19

My Consolation

When my heart is full of burdens,
And I wear my careworn face,
You lift all the weight from my shoulders,
Replacing it with your grace.

Lord You're my one consolation,
You fill me with great cheer,
I need not continue to worry,
For you are always near.
Now if I could only remember,
I need not have cares at all,
For you always stand ready to take them,
All we need do, is call.

So give me a gentle reminder,
To carry within my heart,
You are in charge of my worries,
Oh Master, how great Thou art!

10/01/02

Thou wilt keep him in perfect peace,
whose mind is stayed on Thee.
Trust ye in the Lord forever;
for in the Lord Jehovah
is everlasting strength.
Isaiah 26: 3-4 (KJV).

I Am Blessed!

The Lord fills me with inner peace,
He gives to me great strength.
For I walk with Him daily,
And we speak at great length.

I place my trust in Jesus,
He knows my every need,
Jesus loves and cares for me,
I am blessed indeed.

10/01/02

You Are Always There

When my cup of hope is empty,
I raise it heavenward.
When my courage is lost,
You return it to me.
When my faith
begins to stumble and fall,
You take my hand,
and walk with me.

When all I see are storms,
You paint a bow of colours
In my sky.
When all I see is cruelty,
You show me your love,
in the face of a dying man.

When all I feel is the pain
of a troubled mind,
You send me the soothing ointment
of a robin's song.

When my heart is broken,
You bind it with satin ribbons.
When my spirit seems crushed,
You open the windows of heaven.
And fill me with warmth,
and renew my strength.

For all of these things,
I thank you, Lord.

10/01/02

In His Mercy

In His mercy
And compassion,
He shall reach down
And rescue me.

My suffering
Will not be
Forever.
The Lord's love
Wraps itself around me
As a blanket,
Made of the finest wool.
His bitter cup
Has been sweetened for me.
And served by His loving hand.

With His own holy robe,
He dries my tears,
And brushes back
The hair
from my care worn face.

His love shines upon me
As the hot summer sun,
And I cry no more.

I am blessed.
I am healed.
I am His.

10/01/02

In His Mercy

In His mercy
and compassion,
He shall reach down
and rescue me.

My suffering
will not be
forever.

The Lord's love
wraps itself around me
as a blanket,
made of the finest wool.

His bitter cup
has been sweetened for me
and served by His loving hand.

With His own holy robe,
He dries my tears,
and brushes back
the hair
from my care worn face.

His love shines upon me
as the hot summer sun,
and I cry no more.

I am blessed.
I am healed.
I am His.

10/01/02

I Seek Thee Lord

I seek Thee, Lord,
come talk to me,
bind up this broken heart.

Be my comfort,
and my shield,
give me a brand new start.

Lift me to Your mighty hills,
keep me 'neathe Angels' wings,
fill me with Your spirit, Lord,
teach me how to sing.

I wish to be Your servant,
to do all that You will,
I wish to meet
the needs of all
beside the waters, still.

Tell me of
Your majesty
Of wonderful things to come,
speak to me,
of what will be,
when you take me home.

10/01/02

The Lords' Love

Once upon a time,
a long, long time ago,
when I was just a child,
I felt my father's glow.

I did not understand,
this love I held within,
but I was always certain,
that it came from Him.

The Lord has been so good to me,
as I've moved along the way.
I am His child, His precious one,
and in my heart, He'll stay.

I speak with Him each morning,
to Him I bid, "good night,"
I stay within His loving arms,
He is my guiding light.

If you don't know your father,
I pray you ask Him now,
to come and live
within your heart,
just go to. Him and bow.

Ask Him to forgive you
for all your sins my friend,
He will lift and love you,
your joy shall never end.

10/01/02

The Birds

The birds
sing their praises
to the Lord of life.
He walks
through the garden,
in morning,
while the grass
is still wet with the dew.

The birds
encircle Him in flight,
perching upon His shoulder.
singing their love
into His attentive ear.

Oh to be one of those birds!
To be carried upon
the shoulder of the Lord!
One day,
I shall fly to Him,
and in turn,
sing of my love
and thanksgiving.

Oh what a happy day
That will be!

10/01/02

Whoever serves Me must follow Me;
and where I am, my servant
also will be. My Father will
honor the one who serves me.
1 Cor. 12 27-28
John 12:26

I Follow

I follow my shepherd daily,
He leads me where I should go,
I follow my shepherd daily,
He warms me with His glow.

I listen as He calls me,
with His gentle voice,
I am safely kept by Him,
my following is my choice.

He teaches me to serve Him,
He teaches me to obey,
I follow my shepherd daily,
it's with Him that I will stay.

10/01/02

Why?

Why do we concern ourselves,
with so much earthly care?
Why do we strive
to stay on earth,
When there's so much pain there?

Wouldn't it be wonderful,
to dwell in perfect peace?
To live in love, and harmony,
where praises never cease?

Imagine life in heaven,
no more sorrow or pain.
Nothing more to struggle for,
everything our gain

If His people, called by His name,
would humble themselves and pray,
we'd be standing
before our Lord,
in our heavenly home today!

1 0/01/02

And the Lord said: "Because he loves me,
I will rescue him. I will protect him,
for he acknowledges My name.
He will call upon Me, and I will answer him,
I will be with him in trouble.
I will deliver him, and honor him.
With long life I will satisfy him,
and show him my salvation."
Psalm 91:14-16

God Is So Good

God is so good!
His blessings are many!
I will proclaim His righteousness.
The Lord God has rescued me,
from the depths of despair.
He is my shield from the enemy.

I cried out to Him
In my desperation,
and He heard my voice.
Praise the Lord!
for His mercy is boundless!

He will take me to
His beautiful home,
and I shall live forever.

The Lord will Grown me,
with His salvation,
Though I was black as night
with sin.

God is so good!
His blessings are many!
I shall worship my God and King forever.

10/01/02

You Promised Me

You promised me,
that You would stay,
through my darkest hour.
When I fear
the cold, dark night,
I feel Your might and power.

You promised me,
that You would be,
my helper and my friend.
And I shall draw,
my strength from You,
even till the end.

You promised me,
that You would feed me,
with Your living bread,
and give me,
a place of peace,
to rest mx weary head.

You promised me
A cold, fresh drink,
from Your eternal spring,
You are my Lord,
my living light,
You are my everything.

10/01/02

Let the words of my mouth,
and the meditations of my heart,
be acceptable in Thy sight 0 Lord,
my strength and my redeemer. Psalm 19:14 (KJV)

My Strength and Redeemer

Oh Lord,
I am a sinner,
trying to obey.
And I falter daily,
while walking in Your way.

I arise each morning,
sing praises from my heart,
I ask that You would walk with me,
and make me as Thou art.

Quickly I am swallowed up
by the world around,
I find that I. am sinking,
and surely I will drown.

I call out in my sorrow
my panic and my fear,
I feel Your loving hand on me,
Your voice I always hear.

You set me back
upon the path,
the way that I should go,
and I praise Your precious name,
and feel Your loving glow.

You are my strength
and my redeemer,
my praises shall not be still.
You will work out
my souls perfection,
according to Your will.

10/01/02

My Victory Song

He heard me call Him through the storm,
He heard my pain and fear.
He drew me in with loving arms,
and dried my every tear.

Praise His name ye people!
He cares so much for you!
What other friend so faithful,
would do, all that He'll do?

He .saved you from the serpent,
and set you on His hill,
His treasures now surround you,
if you'll do His will.

Come unto the Father,
through His precious Son,
the battle-flow is over,
the victory He has won.

10/01/02

My Every Prayer

Jesus hears my every prayer,
He answers one by one.
I just walk along with Him,
from sun to setting sun.

His answer is not always yes,
It is not always no,
But He leads me lovingly,
in the way that I should go.

My Shepard feeds me with His word,
He gives me daily bread,
I am strengthened by His love,
and given new paths to tread.

So, I travel, down life's road,
but I don't walk alone,
My Lord is here,
He leadeth me,
To my heavenly home.

10/01/02

My Every Prayer

Jesus hears my every prayer,
He answers one by one.
I just walk along with Him,
from sun to setting sun.

His answer is not always yes,
It is not always no,
but He leads me lovingly,
in the way that I should go.

My shepard feeds me with His word,
He gives me daily bread,
I am strengthened by His love,
and given new paths to tread.

So, I travel, down life's road,
but I don't walk alone,
my Lord is here,
He leadeth me,
to my heavenly home.

10/01/02

Remembering Each Other

We are all His children,
And it's to Him we come,
Remembering each other,
When the day is done.

Jesus knows your every need,
It is for you He cares.
Just go to Him,
You are His child,
He is always there.

10/01/02

You Are My Shelter

You are my shelter in the storm,
you are my strength and shield.
You bring to my life, happiness,
and flowers in my fields.

Though thunder crashes round me,
lightening flashes everywhere,
you hide me neathe
your loving arms,
and I find solice there.

You are my shelter in the storm,
my shield from pain and strife,
You fill the emptiness within,
And guide my daily life.

10/02/02

Come Walk With Me

Come walk with me
in forest green,
come walk with me today.
I long to be with You, my Lord,
I long to learn Your way.

I see Your face, Your presence,
in all with whom I stay,
I search Your word,
your passages,
I hear all that You say.

Come walk with me
in forest green,
come stay with me awhile.
or I am Yours,
my God and King,
I want to be Your child.

10/01/02

Gracious God

O how gracious is our God!
What mercy He bestows!
The seed He plants
within our hearts,
miraculously grows!

It's not that we deserve His love,
for we have done no good.
But He gave it, anyway,
through His son, upon the wood.

O how gracious is our God!
My voice shall praise His name!
He has cleansed, and made me whole,
my life is not the same!

10/01/02

God's Goodness

Gathering the pieces,
of my broken life,
boxing up the sorrow,
the sinfulness and strife.

Thinking back, on empty years,
the misery they brought,
Remembering the ones I hurt,
carelessly, without thought.

It's all too painful to recall,
and yet, somehow, we do.
Often I have wondered,
how do we muddle through.

So many things I wasted,
though I always had a choice,
so much time, gone forever,
save that still small voice.

Gathering the pieces,
I'll remember them no more,
for I know, My loving God,
has so much more in store.

I thank Him for His patience,
His loving, guiding hand,
I thank Him that He sh9wed to me,
His foot prints in the sand.

He never will remember,
the me I used to be,
He only takes. the goodness,
that I have failed to see.

And so I pack the boxes,
of my former self,
I hand them to my savior,
to place upon His shelf.

My guilt and shame I give to Him,
and when I'm through confessing,
He dries my tears,
He softly smiles,
And fills me with His blessing.

10/01102

From Sorrow To Joy

He turned my sorrow, into joy,
my perplexion into peace,
the Lord has blessed me greatly,
my praise shall never cease.

While wandering through the darkness,
weighed down in fear and despair,
the master reassured me,
that He was always there.

Now, we walk together,
from valleys to mountain top,
my praise and prayer,
for Him, who loves me,
shall never, ever stop.

10/01/02

Grace And Glory

Jesus clothed you in grace and glory,
through His death and resurrection.
He placed a crown upon your head,
and made you complete perfection.

The -stripes He wore, upon His flesh,
were meant for you and me.
The spikes that pierced His hands and feet,
were put there to set us free.

Don't you think, that we owe Him,
to always look our best?
Don't *you* think, that how we act,
will reflect that we've been blessed?

Put on your robe of righteousness,
show people your glory and grace,
let the love of Jesus Christ,
shine out, from your face.

It is our duty to honor Him,
to share the love He has given.
· The greatest way to witness,
let others see Him, in your living.

10/01/02

He Leads Me

He leads me through the valleys,
He sets me on the hill.
Everything He owns is mine,
If I will do His will.

He is my umbrella,
my shelter from each storm.
He is my cave and fortress,
I am kept safe 'and warm.

I am His hand-maiden,
He is my teacher, strong.
I walk with Him everywhere,
and praise Him all day long.

When I walk through the darkness,
the caves of deep despair,
all I need do,
is call on Him,
and He is always there.

All l am,
and all I have,
I've given to the King.
He holds me close,
He brings me joy,
and causes my heart to sing!

10/01/02

Blessed Be The Lord

Blessed be the Lord
who rescued me,
from raging,
burning fire.

Blessed be the one
who set me free,
and made me
His desire.

I shall follow,
all my days,
my king and savior true.
He that leads me on His path,
my spirit to renew.

I shall never turn from Him,
He would not let me go.
I shall never see again,
what life of sin and woe.

I am the clay within His hands,
He's working my perfection.
I shall always, ever be,
My Father's true reflection.

10/01/02

51

Praising His Sacrifice

You bore my sins,
O, Precious Lord!
You paid what I
could not afford.

How could You hang
upon that tree,
and give Your life,
for one like me?

The thought of this
I scarce can bare,
the sight of You,
once dying there.

Bring my death,
to earthly sin,
pierce my life,
that I might win.

For my desire is
to be with You,
and greater things yet
shall I do.

I shall declare
over all the earth,
just what is
my savior worth!

All shall bow,
all shall confess,
their sorrow and
their broken-ness.

And then rise,
in voice of praise,
for He shall humble
and amaze.

And when we meet Him,
in the air,
and look upon
that face so fair,

Our voices raise
in victory song,
He paid the price,
our battle is done!

10/01/02

Desire To Serve Him

Lord, make me an instrument
of your perfect peace.
Lay open, my cold, cold heart,
for Your love to release.

Lord, please show compassion,
for the ones I see,
Let Your love and goodness,
shine to them, through me.

Lord, I pray for power,
in all I say and do,
to light the way in darkness,
for salvation to flood through.

Lord, direct my path today,
keep me on steady course,
all glory, praise and honor,
shall forever be Yours.

10l01/02

Psalm 73: 26,28

"...... God is the strength of my heart,
and my portion forever."
"But as for me, it is good to be near God.
I have made the Sovereign Lord my refuge;
I will tell of all Your good deeds."

My Strength And Portion

God is the strength of my heart forever,
He ever my portion shall be.
Locked in a prison of darkness,
He set this captive free.

Now l follow Him daily,
for in me He planted His seeds,
God is the strength of my heart forever,
I will tell of all of His deeds.

Copyright ©1 0/01 2002

The Treasures Of His Kingdom

In this uncertain world,
we all need hope to see,
things will work out,
when it's time,
when it's meant to be.

For if your heart is willing,
to go where 'ere He leads,
He will bless you daily,
you will do mighty deeds.

The treasures of His kingdom,
are yours to have and hold.
Valleys made of silver,
mountains of purest gold.

For when your heart,
belongs to Him,
you've no need of earthly things,
He will give great gifts to you,
sent upon Angel's wings.

My pockets may be empty,
no bank account have I,
but great riches, wait for me;
beyond the day I die.

The heaven's gates will open,
I will be welcomed in,
my life of glory,
with my Lord,
is now to begin.

Take His hand today my friend,
please do not hesitate,
for I shall wait to greet you,
at my master's gate.

10/01/02

"Nothing will be impossible for you!"
Matthew 17:20

Nothing Impossible

He said, that I,
could do all things,
If I would just believe.
He said, all I need do
is ask,
and prepare to receive.

Of course, the road is bumpy,
it won't be always straight,
but He smooths out
the pathways,
of those willing
to wait.

He said,
greater things yet than these,
will I let you do,
follow Me, and trust in Me,
and I will see you through.

If you truly love me,
you'll follow my command,
you shall never walk alone,
I'll always hold your hand.

To my Father be the glory,
in all you say and do,
it is just as I promised,
nothing will be impossible
for you.

10/01/02

Understanding Heart

O, Lord, hear your servant,
from me, do not depart,
I ask that you would give to me,
an understanding heart.

Fill me with compassion,
for my fellow man,
instill in me,
a humble spirit,
as only you can.

Lord, make me an instrument,
of Your perfect peace.
Give command,
all knees shall bow,
the fighting would all cease.

Lord give to me a mission,
to do Your perfect will.
Let me serve Thee,
day by day,
till in death, I be still.

And when I stand before You,
upon Your judgment throne,
let the words,
from Your lips be,
"good job child, welcome home."

10/01/02

I Am His Sheep

I am His sheep,
He leadeth me,
beside the water still.

He leads me
softly, gently,
bidding I do His will.

His rod and staff
my comfort be,
His voice I know so well.
I am His sheep,
He leadeth me,
my love for Him
I'll tell.

He leadeth me from valley,
to the mountain top,
my praise of Him
forever rings,
it shall never stop.

10/01/02

To Be With Him

Oh, to be with Him daily,
to go where ever. He'll be,
oh, to wake in the morning,
and His face, the first thing I see.

How lovely to dine with the Master,
to break bread and drink fine wine,
to sit and talk
the day away,
such a wish is mine.

To sit at the feet of Jesus,
and learn all there is to know,
oh, to be with Him daily,
having Him help me to grow.

10/01/02

Jesus Knows

Jesus knows our every need,
for He was once a man.
So many things we fail at,
Yet, Jesus always can.

"Let not your heart be troubled,"
never be afraid,
He has all of your needs in His care,
for you, the way, He's made.

There is no heart's desire,
that Jesus can not fulfill,
if you give your life to Him,
and heed His perfect will.

Only trust Him completely,
it is your only task,
all of your needs are provided,
if only you will ask.

10/01/02

Special Friend

I have a friend so special,
He is so close to me,
we walk together daily,
there's no place I'd rather be.

With My Friend there's laughter,
and with Him, never fear,
He has watched me
grow and change,
more fully year after year.

My friend will never leave me,
He lives within my soul;
He made me pure as sunshine,
when my sins were black as coal.

The friend I speak of is Jesus,
there is no friend so true,
ask Him into your life today,
and. He'll be your friend too.

10/01/02

My Father's House

My Father's house is beautiful,
and filled with treasures, rare.
I love to go and visit Him,
I feel so safe there.

My Father always welcomes me,
with a loving smile,
He's never in a hurry,
so I stay for awhile.

We stroll the rolling meadows,
the grass so thick, and green.
He lets me pick the flowers,
more colour, I've never seen.

He takes me to
the water's edge,
I can see my reflection.
Despite the many flaws I have,
He tells me I'm perfection.

My Father's house is beautiful,
and filled with treasures rare,
I love to go and visit Him,
I am so loved there.

10/01/02

My "Quilt"

He is my quilt and comforter,
when I am feeling Fear,
He wraps Himself
around me,
and holds me very near.

I close my eyes,
and I can feel,
my head upon His chest.
When I am down,
I go to Him,
He.always knows what's best.

He speaks to me
so softly,
and I listen
with my heart,
He tells me
I am His forever,
never will we part.

He is my quilt and comforter,
no truer friend I know,
He fills my spirit,
with His love,
and sets my heart aglow.

10/01/02

A Prayer To Serve

Lord, make me an instrument
of Your perfect peace,
give to me,
a word to say,
all argument would cease.

Lord. make me a vessel,
fill me with Your love.
Shine through me,
to all I see,
with radiance from above.

Lord. make me a servant,
that I may do Your will,
let me comfort broken hearts
and make .the storms be still.
Lord, make me
a loyal guard,
standing at Your gate,
bringing home Your children,
let me navigate.

Lord, just let me serve you,
this is all I ask,
whether it
be great or small,
I'll take on any task.

10/01/02

The House of God

I went into the house of God,
to be alone with Him.
There were candles burning,
the lights were very dim.

Soft music was arising
sweet to the Angels ears.
All my sorrows lifted,
washed .by my own tears.

My Fathers' hand
had lifted them
from deep within my heart,
He washede me clean,
He made me whole,
I received a brand new start.

Departing from
the house of God,
I had not one care.
How light my spirit now appeared,
as if walking on air.
When you have a burden,
take it to the Lord.
To live in pain and sorrow,
no one can ill afford.

10/01/02

The Sunshine

You let me see the sunshine,
after every storm,
when my heart, is feeling cold,
Your touch will make it warm.

I know that you will walk with me,
through valleys of fear and pain,
I know that You are with me,
through every driving rain.

Now and then, You let me see,
the majestic mountain top.
All the beauty, waiting there,
the reasons I can't stop.

With my shoulder, to the wind,
I make my way along,
You make my journey easier,
You fill my heart with song.

10/01/02

Poetry of Prayer

Oh Lord, My Lord

Oh Lord, my Lord,
I am so weary.
I shake to my very soul,
from fear of that
which I can not see.

There is so much before me.
People look to me
and I have no guidance to offer them.
People see me as
a tower of strength and wisdom,
yet, in my heart,
I feel foolish and spent.

What am I to do, Lord?
I feel empty inside.
My will is depleted.
I feel hopeless and lost.

Come to me, my Lord.
Let me drink from Your cup.
Fill me with Your healing,
loving waters.

Oh Lord, my Lord,
rest is what I need.
Let me rest my troubled head,
upon Your loving shoulder.
Let me. listen,
to the beating, of your
tender heart

I will be filled once again.
I will be refreshed and new.
I will once again put on,
the armor of Your righteousness.

Oh Lord, my Lord,
even though I, am a
soldier for You,
let me still be a child.
Your child.

02/17/04

"Teach us to number our days,
aright,
that we may gain a heart of
wisdom."
Psalm 90:12

Teach us To Number Our Days

The days,
pass quickly by,
the nights,
are but a moment.

Busy minds,
run helter-skelter,
but find no peace
or rest.

The grey hairs come,
the wrinkles increase,
laughter fades
from our lives.

No joy we find,
in the world we know.
No solitude remains
in our souls.

Running here,
rushing there,
making plans,
setting goals, to no avail.

What have we in the end?
Empty hearts,
empty wallets,
and a soul waxing with unrest.

Teach us, Lord,
to number our days.
Help us to create riches
that will endure the pain of life.

May each moment,
be precious,
may your peace,
fill our hearts.

-As long as we can,
see the sun rise in morning,
let us praise your holy name,
for you are the giver of this great gift.

As surely as the stars,
dance in the night sky,
you are there,
walking through the darkness with us.

Teach us Lord,
to celebrate your great gifts,
and to refocus our hearts,
on the beauty around us.

Remove from us,
the shades of despair,
that the colours of our world,
will come shining through.

Lord, open our eyes,
draw us near,
comfort our weary souls.
And most of all...
teach us to number our days,
aright,
that we might gain
a heart of wisdom

·November 9, 2003

Better Would It Be

Better would it be,
to spend one day with Thee,
than to stay a thousand years
upon this earth.

Better would it be,
that I could follow Thee,
and one day learn the fullness
of my worth.

Savior you are dear,
and to you I draw near,
you are my teacher
and my great salvation.

Better this I know,
'tis seeds of faith to grow,
while you prepare for me
my reservation

06/29/03

"Keep your heart with all diligence,
for out of it springs the issues of life ...
Ponder the paths of your feet."
Proverbs 4: 23, 26

Where Will You Send Me?

Where will you send me today, 0 Lord?
For I stand ready to serve.
You have given me wonderful gifts,
none of which I deserve.

Light up my pathway that I may see,
which way you would have me to go.
Open a gift, from deep in my heart,
and watch how it quickly grows.

Cradle my heart in your loving hands,
for it belongs to you,
keep it in purity, that people may see,
your love .shine.in all that I do.

06/21/03

Which Gift?

Which gift, O Lord,
will you use today?
And why have you given me,
so many from which to choose?

Shall I honor you with
the gift of my words?
Yet not my words,
but the words of the Spirit
that dwell within me.

Will you require
the gift of compassion?
The one that
tears at my very heart,
at the sight of all suffering.

Perhaps you will use,
my gift of good listening.
Will you send someone my way?
A soul with a broken heart?
Well, Lord,
I stand ready, gift in hand.

Will you use the gift of
discernment?
Keeping me from being drawn away
by some evil one?
Keeping me on your precious path?

I love your good gifts, Lord.
Every day, you give to me,
a new one to share.
And you return,
time and again,
to share them with me, your daughter.

Which gift will you use today, O Lord?

06/21/03

Set Me Free

Set me free, dear Father,
if it be Thy will,
I am tired of illness
tired of taking pills.

The ups and downs, get so old,
and drive all my loved ones away.
If it be alright with You,
please take this cup away.

But perhaps, you have a plan,
that I don't see as clear,
if it be so, I ask you now,
just by my side stay near..

The road in life can be so long,
the night can be so cold,
but I know that I will make it,
if your hand I can hold.

12/12/03

The Walk

Sighs of sorrow
from deep within,
another day
I must begin.
"Father forgive me,
for I have sinned.
Open Your heart,
let this child in.

This lonely path
I walk each day,
beneathe a cold,
dark sky of gray.
Prayers of anguish
rise to you,
"Please, dear Father,
my life renew."

Taking my hand,
You walk by my side,
'neathe Your mighty wing
I hide.
When I am weak
you carry me,
deliver me safely
please set my heart free.

02-19-03

Silly Bedtime Song

Now I lay me down to sleep,
safely at the masters' feet.
If I toss and turn tonight,
I will be within His sight,

He will comfort
my broken heart,
because from me,
He'll never part.

He sings me songs,
and strokes my head,
and tucks me safely,
into bed.

I love my master,
from above,
He bathes me in
His wonderful love.

What Can I Do?

What can I do for you today
my precious Lord and King?
You have saved and made me whole,
I owe you everything.

Could I be your candle
burning bright in someone's' storm?
Perhaps I'll show compassion
to keep a sad heart warm.

Will you let me be the one
to lead a soul to you?
Will you teach me how to let
your love come shining through?

What can I do for you today
for my life has no needs,
I could be your gardener,
and plant loves'. precious seeds.

10/01/02

Bravity

God please grant me bravity
To weather storms that come to me.
I don't ask you keep me from them,
I only wish to rise above them.

When my life, seems dark and cold,
I'll reach up, your hand to hold.
When my fears seem to surround me,
I'll feel your loving arms around me.

09/10/02

Father of Lights

"Every good gift and every perfect gift is from above,
and comes down from the Father of lights.
James 1:17 (NKJV)

It's not what we have, but how we use it.

Father of lights shine down on me,
Shower me with your mercy.
Father of hope rain down on me,
Let me your servant be.

Cleanse my hands and my heart, O Lord,
Ready them for your use.
That I might reach out in love to others,
And free them from Satan's abuse

Father, please clear any clouds from my eyes,
That I might fully see,
All of the beautiful gifts you have given,
Blessings you've shown to me.

Show me dear Lord, as I go through this day,
Someone who needs your care.
So I may take the gifts you have given,
And with someone openly share.

Help me to show someone heart to heart,
that these gifts have come from you.
That they would ask you into their lives,
And receive your love and gifts too.

Oh how I praise you, dear Father of lights,
And all that you've done for me,
Now let me pass on these wonderful gifts,
That others will see you in me.

08/21/02

God Why Can't I Be Normal?

Here I sit again,
Tears streaming down my face.
Why must I continue,
In this sorrowful place?

All my dreams in pieces,
Friendships shattered too,
God, why can't you tell me,
What I'm supposed to do?

Is there some great reason,
That we should suffer so?
Will I ever get to bask,
In Your loving glow?

God, I want to be normal!
That's all I ask of You.
God, why can't be normal?
I want to be happy too!

Comfort My Heart

Dear Lord,
Please come,
And comfort *my* heart.
I lay the pieces at your feet.

I can not contain the tears,
Nor can I hold the pain any longer.
Lord, please do not leave me
Here in this place of desolation.

My bones are separating
My muscles are being stripped from me.
I lay raw, open,
bleeding within my soul.

Lord, please reach down
just now,
And touch your suffering child.
As you have promised in your word.

Please help me
To rise again
Renew my strength.
Replenish my trust in you,
And in others.

Lord, it is You
And you alone in whom
I place *my* trust.
You are *my* stronghold.

It is by your mighty hand
That I am delivered
from mine enemies.
Thanks be to God!

You will raise me,
And cleanse me,
And make me whole again,
According to the promises of your word.

I thank you, O rock of my salvation.
Amen.

10/01/02

The Language Of Sorrow

The language of sorrow
Is understood,
By all who have felt the pain.

Heart to heart
We can be heard,
When traveling
Through the rain.

The Lord had great compassion,
For those who sorely grieved.
His tenderhearted mercy,
All of their pain relieved.

When my brother is broken,
His language of sorrow I hear.
I feel his pain,
In my own heart,
Whether he be far or near.

The language of sorrow
Is understood,
It needs no interpretation,
The touch of one
Who has known the pain,
Is another's form of salvation

You Are Always There

When my cup of hope is empty,
I raise it heavenward.
When my courage is lost,
You return it to me.
When my faith
begins to stumble and fall,
You take my hand,
And walk with me.

When all I see are storms,
You paint a bow of colours
In my sky.
When all I see is cruelty,
You show me your love,
In the face of a dying man.

When all I feel is the pain
Of a troubled mind,
You send me the soothing ointment
Of a robin's song.

When my heart is broken,
You bind it with satin ribbons.
When my spirit seems crushed,
You open the windows of heaven.
And fill me with warmth
And renew my strength.

or all of these things,
I thank you, Lord.

10/01/02

"And the God of all grace,
who called you to His eternal glory in Christ,
after you have suffered for a little while,
will Himself restore you and make you strong,
firm, and steadfast. 1 Peter 5:10 (NIV)

Rescue Me

How long, O Lord,
before my strength returns?
I am so weary
and downhearted.

Will it be a day,
which is as a thousand years?
Oh to return
to the confidence of my youth!
To wear a smile again,
and feel it's glow
deep within my heart.

My faith is shaken
Merciful Father.
I have death grip
on my sanity.
That still, small voice,
whispers: "hold on!"
But for how long,
Precious Lord?
Rescue me today,
I pray.

10/01/02

One thing I ask of the Lord,
this is what I seek:
that I may dwell in the house of the Lord all the days of my life,
to gaze upon the beauty of the Lord
and to seek Him in His temple.
Psalm 27:4 KJV

Patience

I dream of heaven.
How I long to be there!
The world is such
a cold, dark place!

Everywhere I look,
I see the pain.
I cry unto the Lord.
"Patience", He replies.
How many days
must I wait?
Why won't people
lay down their hatred?
Why won't they exchange their weapons
for instruments of peace?

Oh, how I long,
to look into the face of Jesus!
Love pouring from His eyes.
Gentle affection He speaks,
to my heart.
He soothes my troubled mind
With the balm of His love.
And speaks but one word…..
Patience

Come to Me all you who are weary and
burdened, and I will give you rest.
Matthew 11:28 NIV

Where Is The Rest?

I'm so tired, Lord!
Where is the rest
that You have promised?
My bones ache!
My heart aches!
There is wickedness everywhere!

We live in a world
gone mad, Lord!
Brother consumes brother.
What were once considered to be
unspeakable acts,
are now considered pleasure!
People who were once held,
in highest regard.
are now the most wretched. sinners of all!

I come to You, Lord.
asking, "when?"
When will the burdens
of sin be lifted?
When will we cry out no more?
I'm so tired, Lord!
Where is the rest
that You have promised?

10/01/02

He gave His life

He gave His life,
Upon a tree,
This gentle man
From Galilee.

He bled and died,
To save and free,
A wretched sinner
Such as me.

And just what things
Have I done,
To claim the victory
Of the Son?

How often have
I turned away,
Not knowing
Just what to say?

How often now
Have I shut down,
And found my spirit
On the ground?

Have I put
His death to waste,
In all I fear,
In such great haste?
Reach down to me
O Precious One.
Please fix the things
That I have done.

Please do not hide
Your face from me,
But forever
My comfort be.

Close my mouth,
Open my heart,
Help me to be,
All. that thou art,
Your precious blood
That was shed,
Will now cleanse
My sorrowed head.

I wish to walk
Along with You
Show me, Master,
What to do.

10/01/02

Printed in the United States
By Bookmasters